Contents

All change

Do your parents like to embarrass you by showing off your baby photos? Next time they do this, take a quick look if you dare. Can you recognise yourself?

Can you see how much you've changed? Since the day you were born, your body has been changing and these changes carry on through your life. Sometimes the changes are too small to notice, but sometimes they can make you feel as if you're turning into a creature from another planet!

One of the times when you change the most is called puberty. This is when you go from being a child to being an adult. Your body changes on the outside and on the inside. You might have noticed some of these changes happening already. They might be happening to your friends, but not to you. Don't worry. Puberty is different for everyone and can happen at different times and speeds.

Puberty is a completely normal and natural part of growing up. While it's happening to you, it can feel scary, confusing, irritating and embarrassing. The changes that are happening in puberty not only affect you physically, they also change the way you feel and behave, and how you get on with your family and friends. This book will help you understand more about what is happening to you.

More about puberty

During puberty, your body changes from a boy's into a man's, ready for your adult life. Some of these changes mean you'll be able to be a father one day, if you wish to.

Your body changes because your brain starts to make powerful chemicals, called hormones. Your blood carries these hormones to different parts of your body. Some hormones control how your body uses energy; some instruct your body to grow. During puberty, the most important hormone in your body is testosterone. It causes changes to your sex organs, so that, in time, you'll be able to start a family.

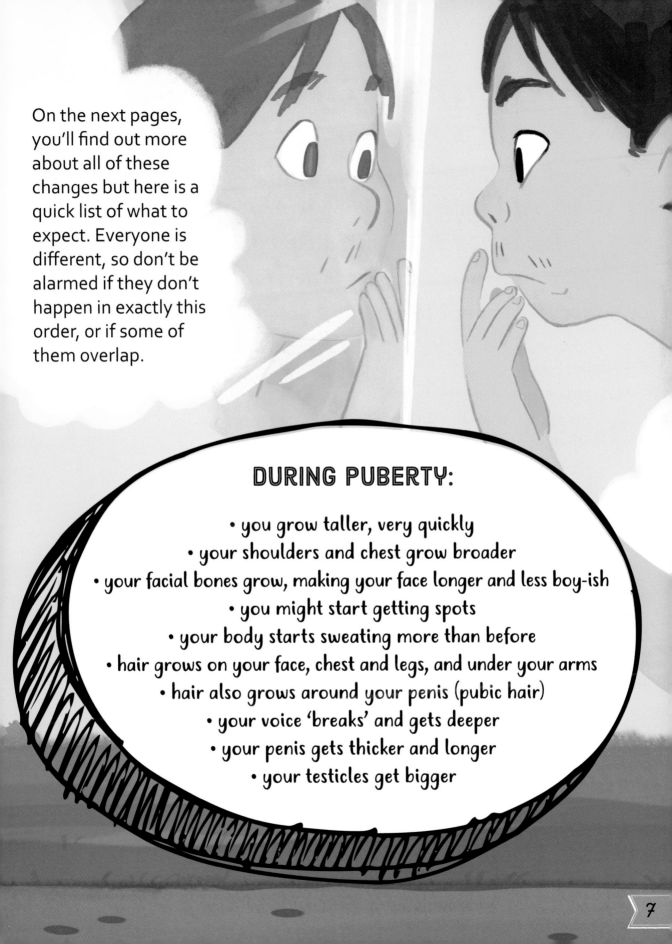

On the next pages, you'll find out more about all of these changes but here is a quick list of what to expect. Everyone is different, so don't be alarmed if they don't happen in exactly this order, or if some of them overlap.

DURING PUBERTY:

- you grow taller, very quickly
- your shoulders and chest grow broader
- your facial bones grow, making your face longer and less boy-ish
- you might start getting spots
- your body starts sweating more than before
- hair grows on your face, chest and legs, and under your arms
- hair also grows around your penis (pubic hair)
- your voice 'breaks' and gets deeper
- your penis gets thicker and longer
- your testicles get bigger

Changing times

For boys, puberty can happen at any age between 11 and 15 years old. Don't worry if it seems as if all your friends are changing, but not much is happening to you. Everyone develops at different speeds – try not to compare yourself.

Girls go through puberty, too, and their bodies change in lots of different ways. This usually happens between the ages of 8 and 13 years. Like boys, girls get taller and grow more hair on their bodies. They start to grow breasts and their periods begin. The changes that girls go through make it possible for them to have babies in the future.

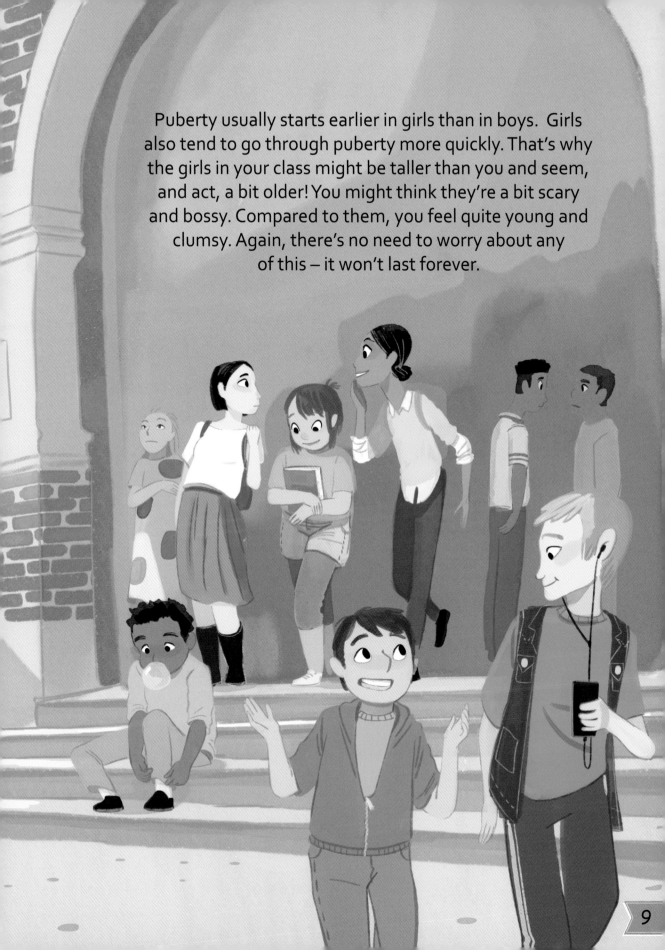

Puberty usually starts earlier in girls than in boys. Girls also tend to go through puberty more quickly. That's why the girls in your class might be taller than you and seem, and act, a bit older! You might think they're a bit scary and bossy. Compared to them, you feel quite young and clumsy. Again, there's no need to worry about any of this – it won't last forever.

Shaping up

Your body shape changes during puberty. One of the first signs you might notice is that you grow taller, quite quickly, but not all of you grows at the same rate. Your hands and feet get bigger, then your arms and legs get longer. This can feel very strange, at first, as if your limbs don't belong to you anymore. Your arms and legs might also ache.

At the same time, your shoulders and chest grow broader. You may also get heavier as your muscles begin to develop. This growth spurt can last for several years, and can be tricky to get used to as it happens. One week, your favourite shirt fits perfectly. The next, the sleeves barely reach past your elbows and the collar is way too tight.

There's so much going on during puberty that it's easy to feel self-conscious and worry about how you look. You might feel jealous of a friend who is skinnier than you, or who has bigger muscles. It's easy to get hung up on your appearance when you are changing so much. Just remember, most likely, your friends are all feeling the same.

WHY AM I SO CLUMSY?

As your body changes, you might find you keep knocking things over, or tripping up. This is quite normal as the rest of your body catches up and adjusts to the new you.

Highs and lows

One day, you're speaking quite normally, the next, your voice starts to crack. One minute, it's higher than usual; another, it sounds like a growl. People keep telling you that your voice is 'breaking'. What on earth is going on?

The larynx (voice box) in your throat is where your voice comes from. Two muscles, called vocal cords, stretch across your larynx, like rubber bands. When you speak, you breathe out and air rushes over the cords. The air makes the cords wobble, and make sounds.

When you're young, your larynx is quite small, and your vocal cords are short and thin. They make higher sounds. As you go through puberty, your larynx gets bigger and your vocal cords become longer and thicker. This gives you a stronger, deeper voice.

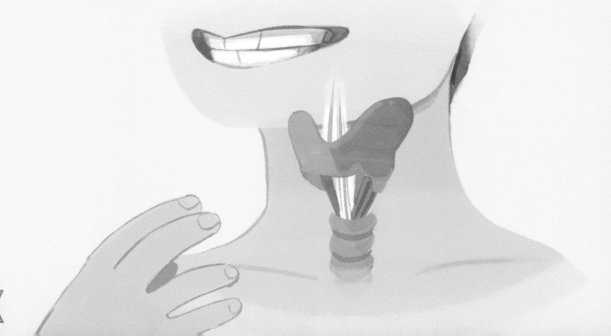

Your new voice can take a bit of getting used to. As your larynx grows and your body adjusts, it can be difficult to control your voice. You might find yourself talking in a squeak one minute, then growling or croaking the next. Don't panic – it's nothing to be embarrassed about. Once your larynx has finished growing, all these odd noises will settle down.

WHAT'S THIS BIG BUMP IN MY THROAT?

It's called your Adam's apple, and it's nothing to worry about. As your larynx gets bigger, it tilts at an angle, and part of it sticks out at the front of your throat.

Hair everywhere

One sure sign puberty has begun is that you start to get hairier. There's no set age for this to happen, so don't worry if you're not as hairy as your friends. As grown-ups, some men are hairier than others – it's different for everyone.

One of the first places you might notice hair sprouting is around your penis. These short, coarse, curly hairs are called pubic hairs. They may grow towards your tummy button as you get older. Hair also appears in your armpits and may also grow on your chest and back. Again, some boys grow thick hairs on their chest, while others are hardly hairy at all.

About two years after your pubic hair appears, hair begins to grow on your face. The first hairs may appear at the corners of your upper lip and then spread across your lip. They then spread to the upper parts of your cheeks below bottom lip, and finally to the sides of your face and chin. These hairs may get thicker and darker over time. This is when you may need to start shaving (see page 16).

WHEN CAN I GROW A BEARD?

Boys are usually close to the end of puberty before they can grow a full beard. Then, some can grow thick, heavy beards while others can grow only a few whiskers.

Starting to shave

Learning to shave can be tricky at first, but you'll soon get the hang of it. If you're not sure what to do, try asking your dad or an older brother, friend or cousin for tips. You don't need to start shaving until you're ready.

There are lots of different razors around. You're probably best using a disposable razor to begin with. You might want to try an electric razor later. Never share your razor with anyone. Always make sure that the blade is sharp – a blunt razor can make your skin red and sore.

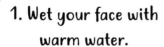

1. Wet your face with warm water.

2. Squirt shaving foam or gel into your hand, then rub it on your face.

3. Try to stretch your skin slightly to make it flat to shave.

4. Shave with long strokes of your razor in the direction the hair grows.

5. Shave your chin and cheeks first, then your upper lip.

6. Rinse your razor regularly to stop it getting clogged with hair.

7. When you've finished, rinse your face with warm water.

8. Clean your razor before and after use.

WHAT IF I CUT MYSELF SHAVING?

It's easy to cut or nick yourself shaving, especially when you start. If this happens, press a clean tissue on your skin to stop any bleeding.

Feeling sweaty

Sweat is a clear liquid that's made in sweat glands in your skin. When it's hot, the glands release sweat on to your skin. The sweat evaporates in the heat, and helps to cool you down. So, sweat is useful, and everyone sweats sometimes.

During puberty, you start to sweat more, especially in your armpits and groin. If the sweat mixes with bacteria on your skin, it can start to smell. This smell is known as B.O. (short for body odour), and it really pongs. To avoid B.O., try to have a bath or shower every day, especially if you've been doing sport. You can use a deodorant under your arms to stop them smelling. Change your clothes often and wear a clean shirt to school every day.

Your armpits aren't the only parts of your body that might start to smell. Your feet can also pong. This is because bacteria in your socks and shoes mix with sweat, especially if you've been on your feet all day long. Then when you take your shoes off and the smell can be terrible.

To stop your feet from stinking, try to wash them every day and make sure you dry them properly. Don't wear the same shoes all the time, especially not if they're trainers, which make your feet sweat more. You can also buy special insoles to put in your shoes that help to combat smells.

HOW OFTEN SHOULD I CHANGE MY SOCKS?

Change your socks every day or if they get damp. Cotton socks are a good choice because they let your feet breathe, and soak up sweat.

Spots and stuff

If smelly feet weren't enough, you're also likely to get spots on your face and body, too. Spots can make you feel down or self-conscious, but you're not alone – at least nine out of ten boys (and girls) get them during puberty. So, what are spots and how do you get them? It's those pesky hormones at work again.

Your skin makes a kind of oil, called sebum. Sebum helps to keep your skin soft and waterproof. Most of the time, your skin makes just the right amount of sebum, but during puberty your hormones tell your skin to make more sebum. This extra oil can clog up the pores in your skin and cause spots to appear. Some spots are tiny and painless. However, if bacteria mixes with the sebum, spots can become red and sore.

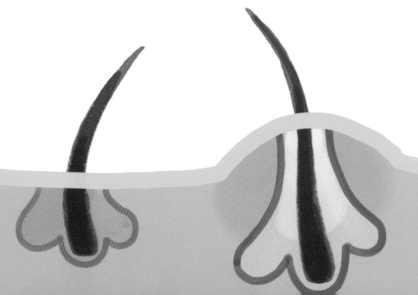

You might hear lots of other reasons why spots happen. Don't listen – they're not true! You don't get spots from eating greasy food and you can't catch spots from someone else. The best thing is not to get too upset or worried about spots, because stress might make spots worse!

HOW CAN I GET RID OF MY SPOTS?
Turn the page! On the next two pages, there's lots of advice for you.

Skin and hair care

The good news is that spots usually don't last long and clear up for good after puberty. In the meantime, there are lots of things you can do to keep your skin healthy and your spots under control.

- Wash your face twice a day with warm water and mild soap or cleanser.

- Pat your skin dry - don't scrub. Scrubbing can make spots worse.

- If you have long hair, keep it away from your face.

- Try not to keep touching or picking at your face.

- If you've got spots on your chest or back, wear loose clothes.

- Eat a healthy diet and drink plenty of water.

If you're worried that you get a lot of spots, talk to your parents. You might need a cream or lotion specially designed to help young skin. You can buy some of these spot treatments from the chemist, or ask your doctor for advice. There's no need to be embarrassed. The sooner you can get your spots sorted, the better you'll feel.

The same oil that causes spots can make your hair greasier than before. You might also need to wash it every day and get a shampoo for greasy hair.

IS IT OKAY TO SQUEEZE MY SPOTS?

No, you could make them worse! You might squeeze bacteria into them and make them last longer. There's also the risk of leaving tiny scars on your skin.

Boys' bits

During puberty, your sex organs develop and grow. You'll notice that your penis (willy) gets longer and thicker, and your testicles (balls) get bigger. Your testicles also start to make tiny cells called sperm, so you can be a father one day.

Your penis does two main jobs. It lets you get rid of urine when you go for a pee. It also passes sperm into a woman's body so it can join with an egg cell. When a sperm and egg cell join they form an embryo, which grows into a baby. Sperm squirts out of the end of your penis in white, sticky fluid, called semen.

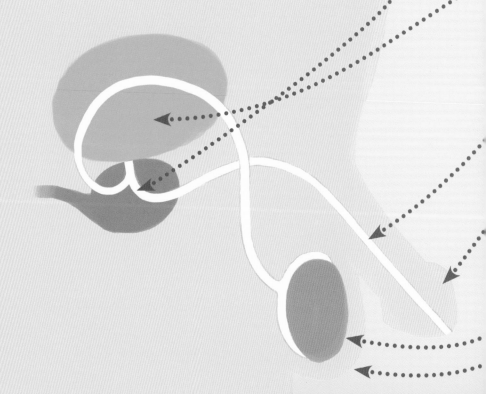

URETHRA

A tube that carries urine from your bladder to your penis.

SPERM DUCTS

Tiny tubes that carry sperm from your testicles to your penis.

FORESKIN

A fold of skin that covers the sensitive tip of your penis.

BLADDER

A bag of muscle that stores urine until you're ready to go for a pee.

TESTICLES

Your two testicles make and store millions of tiny sperm cells. They also make testosterone.

SCROTUM

The wrinkly bag of skin that hangs below your penis, and holds your testicles.

IS MY PENIS TOO SMALL?

Many boys worry about this but most likely, your penis is a normal size. Penises vary in shape and size and don't stop growing until you're about 18.

Soft and hard

Your penis is usually soft and floppy. Sometimes, when you get excited, it can become stiff and stick out from your body. This is called an erection. Extra blood flows into your penis, making it longer and harder.

You might get an erection if you're thinking about a girl or boy that you fancy, but sometimes it happens for no reason at all. You might get an erection when you don't expect it – on the bus or at your desk at school. This can be a bit embarrassing – your penis seems to have a life of its own. If you're worried that someone will notice, hold your school bag or jumper in front of you.

Erections can happen at any time. You might have several in a day, or you have none. They can last for a long or short time. When you get an erection, your penis might be slightly curved or bent. All of this is completely normal. Most of the boys in your class are probably going through the same thing – it's nothing to worry about.

WHY DO I WAKE UP WITH AN ERECTION?

Because you're normal! Erections are very common in the morning.

Wet dreams

Some mornings, you might wake up and find wet patches on your sheets or pyjamas. Don't panic – you haven't wet yourself in the night. It's called a wet dream and it happens because you ejaculate in your sleep. This means that semen squirts out of your penis.

Usually, wet dreams happen if you are having a dream about someone you fancy. You might wake up in the middle of it, but most likely, you'll sleep right through. Having a wet dream can feel strange and confusing, but remember, most boys have them at some time. There is nothing to feel embarrassed or even guilty about. Wet dreams happen less as you get older and your body gets used to all the changes of puberty. In the meantime, wipe your sheets or PJs with some kitchen towel, or pop them in the washing machine.

During puberty, it's a good idea to wash your penis and scrotum every day to keep them clean and healthy. If you get any pain in your penis or it looks red and sore, get it checked by your doctor. You might have an infection and need a cream to clear it up.

A good night's sleep

Puberty is exhausting! It's official. All the changes happening to you use up huge supplies of energy. Then there's going to school, seeing friends and playing sport. No wonder you're tired a lot of the time.

At the end of each day, your body needs to rest and recharge, ready for the next day. This is where a good night's sleep comes in. If you don't get enough sleep during puberty, you'll find yourself getting even more tired (and grumpy!), having problems concentrating and not growing as much as you should. This is because when you sleep, your body makes a hormone that helps you to grow.

Some people need more sleep than others. Ideally, between the ages of 5–12 years, you need around 10 to 11 hours' sleep a night. As a teenager, you need about 9.5 hours. Don't worry if you can't get out of bed in the morning. Scientists have found out that a teenager's sleep patterns are different from young children and adults. So, it doesn't mean that you're lazy – in fact, you're completely normal.

You might also find it tricky dropping off at night. There are lots of things you can do to help you go to sleep, such as being active during the day and going to bed at the same time every night. Turn off your tech at least an hour before you go to bed. Watching TV or being on your phone can make it harder to nod off.

Hunger pangs

During puberty, you'll probably feel hungry nearly all the time. This is because you're growing and changing so fast. Your body is burning up loads of energy and needs refuelling regularly.

The best way to stay healthy is to eat a balanced diet. This will help you to stay at a healthy weight, and to look and feel your best. Eating a balanced diet means eating a mixture of different kinds of food. Try to include lots of fruit and vegetables, and go easy on fatty or sweet foods. It's okay to grab some crisps or a chocolate bar as a treat, but not every day. If you're back from school and starving, try a healthy snack, such as fruit, plain popcorn or a handful of nuts instead.

To wash your balanced diet down, the best thing to drink is water. It'll quench your thirst and keep you healthy. Try to drink around six glasses a day, even if you don't feel thirsty. Fizzy drinks and fruit juice are fine now and again, but they are full of sugar that will rot your teeth if you drink too much of them.

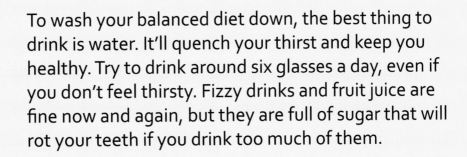

IS FAST FOOD BAD FOR ME?

It can be, if you have it too often. Fast food tastes good, partly because it's high in sugar, fat and salt, which are unhealthy if you eat too much of them.

Feeling fit

You'll find it easier to cope with all the ups and downs of puberty if you keep fit and stay active. Exercise is brilliant for keeping your body strong and at a healthy weight. It will also make you feel better as it cuts down stress and helps you to relax. Exercise releases endorphins, hormones that make you feel happy.

So, how much exercise should you do? If you can, aim for around an hour a day. This sounds like a lot to fit in to your busy life, but you can include walking to school, doing P.E., taking the dog for a walk – anything that gets you moving. Better still, you don't have to do the whole hour in one go. You can split it into shorter bursts of, say, 15 minutes each.

Some boys are super-sporty, others aren't quite so keen. The good news is that exercise doesn't have to mean lifting weights at the gym, or playing in the school team. The trick is to find something you like doing. That way, you're more likely to stick at it and stay motivated. Try varying the things you do, so that you don't get bored. You could also team up with a few friends. You'll keep each other going and have fun at the same time.

DOES WASHING THE CAR COUNT AS EXERCISE?
Yes! Washing the car, mowing the lawn, even tidying your bedroom (if you do it properly) all count as exercise.

Feeling up ... and down

All those hormones rushing around your body have a big effect on your feelings. One minute, you might be feeling on top of the world. The next, you're miserable, but you've no idea why. It's annoying, confusing and even scary, but don't panic. Your emotions are all over the place and that's a completely normal part of growing up. Things will settle down.

As part of your changing moods, you might find it harder to control your temper. You might get angry about things that never bothered you before. The smallest thing makes you lose your cool and you just want everyone to leave you ALONE.

Anger is a normal emotion – everyone gets angry sometimes. It's how you deal with it that's important. When you're in the middle of a temper tantrum, it can be difficult to think straight. The more people tell you to calm down, the angrier you get.

Next time, you get angry, try to breathe deeply, or count to ten, until you feel calmer again. Going for a walk, doing some exercise or listening to your favourite music can also help. It will take time to learn to control anger but keep trying. It will stop you doing things that you might regret later, such as breaking things, shouting or making people feel scared.

Family matters

Are your parents driving you bonkers? Do you wish they'd stop treating you like a child? Do they complain that you're always out with your friends, then moan when you're at home on your phone? Puberty can change your relationships with other people so that it can feel as if the world is going mad.

As you grow up, you desperately want to be treated like an adult, but your parents are still telling you what to do. This can lead to rows at home. The trouble is that you're not grown up yet, and it can be tricky to cope with too much responsibility. Remember, if you want your parents to treat you as a grown up, throwing a tantrum like a toddler won't help!

Your parents love you and want you to be happy. So, why not try to meet them half way? Talk to them about how you feel and take time to listen to their point of view. If you want them to stay out of your room, for example, you could offer to keep it tidy and put your washing outside the door every day.

MY PARENTS WON'T GIVE ME ANY MONEY. WHAT CAN I DO?
Volunteer to do some jobs around the house. You'll earn some money and it will show your parents that you are growing up, too.

Friends and more

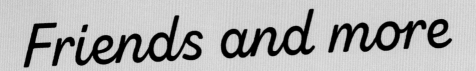

Do your friends keep changing? Have you started fancying someone? During puberty, your circle of friends can change a lot, especially when you move from primary school to secondary school. You'll make new friends, and drop some old ones. Then it can all change again.

The important thing is to work out which friends are good for you and which friends are not. Some might tempt you to to do things you know are wrong, others might ask you to do things you don't really want to do. If they're all doing it, you probably won't want to be the odd one out. This could be something like skiving off school, not doing your homework, or being mean to other people. If this happens, try to stay strong and say 'no'.

You might also start fancying people. Every time you see them, your stomach turns somersaults, but you're too shy to talk to them. It might be a pop star or sports star. You might think about them all the time. For a while, it can seem as if these feelings are taking over your life, but they will calm down.

WHAT IF I LIKE BOYS NOT GIRLS?

Fancying someone of the same sex is quite common during puberty. It's part of working out who you are. If you still like boys when you're older, that's completely fine.

And finally ...

Talk to anyone and they'll all agree – growing up is not easy. It's like riding a rollercoaster, full of extraordinary ups and downs. Just when you think the ride's ending, it starts all over again.

The changes that are happening to you are amazing and life changing, but they're also exhausting and confusing. Hopefully, reading this book will have helped you to understand more about what is happening you, and to feel more confident and positive.

Many boys find it hard to talk about their feelings, or to admit that they're finding things tough. If you are worried about anything, there are always people you can talk to. Talking to your parents can be easier if you're in the car, or kicking a ball about. If this doesn't work for you, try an older brother or sister, a teacher, or a youth worker. If you are really struggling, there are helplines that you can phone. You'll find more information on the next two pages.

By the end of puberty, you'll not only be taller than your parents (probably), but you'll have worked out much more about who and what you are, or want to be. The tricky times won't last for ever so try to enjoy the good bits, and get ready to meet the new you!

Good Luck!

Further advice

We hope that you have found this book useful and that it will help you to understand what puberty is all about. It's important to remember that puberty is a natural, normal part of growing up. If you are worried about anything, though, try talking to your friends. You'll probably find that they're worrying about exactly the same things as you! You could also talk to a trusted adult, such as a parent or carer, teacher, uncle or older brother.

If you don't feel that you can talk to the people around you, there are lots of places that offer advice and help. Here are just a few ...

Websites

www.childline.org.uk
The ChildLine website offers lots of advice and information about all aspects of puberty and growing up. They also run a 24-hour helpline for young people who are having problems.

www.nhs.uk/live-well
This National Health Service website has information about puberty for girls and boys, and videos of teenagers talking about growing up and the ways that they are coping.

www.healthforteens.co.uk
This website has been produced by school nurses, in consultation with young people. It gives advice about how to stay healthy, both physically and mentally, during puberty.

https://kidshealth.org
A brilliant U.S. website, giving lots of useful and accurate information for younger children, teenagers and their parents.

Further reading

Body Positive: A Teenage Guide to a Positive Body Image
by Nicola Morgan (Franklin Watts, 2018)

Healthy for Life series: *Food and Eating/Keeping Fit/Self-esteem and Mental Health* by Anna Claybourne (Franklin Watts, 2018)

Positively Teenage: a positively brilliant guide to teenage well-being
by Nicola Morgan (Franklin Watts, 2018)

Puberty in Numbers: Everything You Need to Know about Growing Up
by Liz Flavell (Franklin Watts, 2019)

The Boy Files: All About Puberty and Growing Up
(Wayland, 2012)

Glossary

Absorbent Made from a material that soaks up liquid easily

Bacteria Microscopic living things that can be helpful or harmful

Breasts Two organs on a woman's chest that can produce milk after childbirth

Body odour A smell caused by sweat mixing with bacteria on your skin. Also called B.O.

Disposable Something that can be used, then thrown away or recycled

Endorphins Hormones that make you feel good

Evaporate To turn from liquid into vapour

Fancy To find another boy or girl very attractive

Glands Organs in the body that release substances either out of the body (for example, sweat, tears), or into the body or bloodstream (for example, hormones)

Groin The part of your body where your legs join your abdomen (trunk)

Growing pains Aches and pains that you might feel as your body grows during puberty

Growth spurt When you get taller over a short period of time during puberty

Hormone A strong chemical that travel around your body in your blood.

Infection When a part of your body is invaded with bacteria or a virus, causing you to feel sore or unwell

Period A few days of bleeding from a girl's body that happens every month

Pore A tiny opening in the skin

Pubic hair Short, wiry hair that grows around your sex organs on the outside of your body

Self-conscious When you feel worried or nervous about what people think of you or how you look

Sex organs The parts of your body that are used to make babies

Sperm A sex cell made in a boy's body

Testosterone A hormone made in a boy's testicles

Urine A liquid made by the kidneys to carry waste products out of your body.

Index